LIFE IS ALWAYS HELD IN EQUILIBRIUM

A Book of Universal Law

Yuki

Yuki's Art & Language

Gold Coast, Australia

Copyright © 2020 by Yuki's Art & Language

All rights reserved. No part of this publication may be reproduced, distributed or transmitted in any form or by any means, without prior written permission.

Yuki's Art & Language
PO Box 3301, Australia Fair
QLD, Australia
www.yukisartandlanguage.com

LIFE IS ALWAYS HELD IN EUILIBRIUM / Yuki's Art & Language. -- 1st ed.
ISBN 978-0-6488108-2-7

Dedication to my daughter and me

Contents

FORM A QUESTION 2
ONE 4
EVERYTHING IN NATURE IS CHANGING 6
LOVE CREATION AND EVOLUTION 8
I AM THE NATURE WITH CONSCIOUSNESS 10
LOVE CREATION AND DEVELOPMENT 12
YOU HOLD THE KEY 14
LIFE JOURNEY 16
NATURAL LAW 18
FREQUENCY 20
HAPPY ECLIPSE ALL CHANGES ARE FOR REBALANCING 22
AUTHENTICITY 24
AVATAR IN TRAINING 26
COM-PASS 28
DOLPHINS AND A DOT 30
WITHOUT DIFFERENCE, THERE IS NO BALANCE & HARMONY ... 32
SUCCESSFUL RELATIONSHIP 34
YIN AND YANG 36
INTER DEPENDANCE IS AN EXPRESSION OF ONENESS 38

FORM A QUESTION

The pool of all there is, the source, is like fluid.

Hold a question as the answer attracts to it.

It is the question that is the lightbulb moment.

What is your question?

Hold it in your mind and wait for the answer to come to you.

Maybe when you are not expecting, possibly through someone or something, somehow, the answer will come to you.

Or you may receive the answer straight away.

Form a question in your mind.

For answers come from the Source.

ONE

One planet.

Another planet.

It's not hard to recognize that the Earth, all that is there, is 'One'.

It is not that complicated when we see it from afar.

'The collective on Earth' is 'One'; therefore, we are 'One'.

As we broaden the scale of our view, it shows itself:

Our solar system seen from afar is 'One'.
Our galaxy seen from afar is 'One'.
Our Universe seen from afar is 'One' and so on.

You see, it is an eternal 'One'.

EVERYTHING IN NATURE IS CHANGING

Everything in nature is changing according to its season, weather, environment, cycle and eco-system.

So we are changing too.

We, humans, are part of nature as we are biological beings.

We change naturally and sometimes consciously.

We are going through different stages in life with the choices we make.

When our heart matures, we are in our fruition.

We are in our element of creation, aligning with the great nature.

Everything in nature is changing.

I AM THE NATURE WITH CONSCIOUSNESS

I am a part of nature.

I am an organic being.

I breathe, drink, eat, sleep and move just like nature, animals and many creatures.

But I also ask questions.

Who am I?

What can I do?

We are always asking questions.

That is consciousness.

It is the ability to think.

But that comes with responsibility.

Great strength comes with great responsibility.

LOVE CREATION AND EVOLUTION

Creation creates.

It continues to create and expand.

Creation only has one agenda. That is to create.

As the Creation keeps creating and expanding, evolution takes place.

Biological adaptability takes place.

It's sometimes subtle, sometimes noticeable, sometimes dramatically metamorphosing.

Creation evolves to adapt.

Every living creation always chooses to live and exist in a better way. So that it can create and expand more of whatever it desires.

LOVE CREATION AND DEVELOPMENT

Creation evolves and develops. While everything naturally evolves, the ability to develop is the power of consciousness.

We humans are conscious beings.

It is an extra component humans have.

Development is the fruition of 'intentional better'.

Development creates more awareness, more adaptability to the changing environment, not just biologically, but also mentally and emotionally.

That is why development's quality depends on a human being's state of mind.

Aligning development with Creation is the key to success.

Love Creation & development.

creation & Love development

YOU HOLD THE KEY

You hold the key to your life; no one else does.

That is your sacred place.

That is your right.

That is your personal space, personal power and the ultimate power.

This key protects you.

It only answers to you, as it respects you.

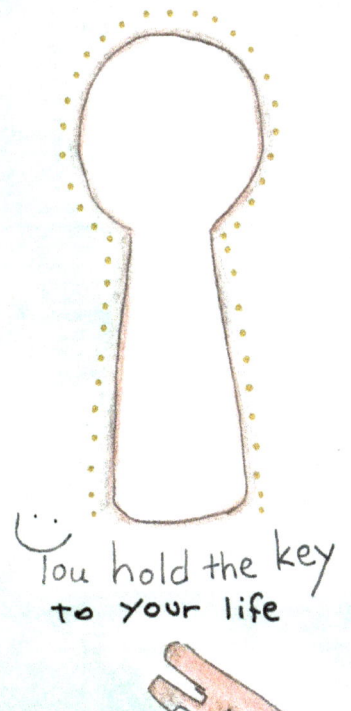
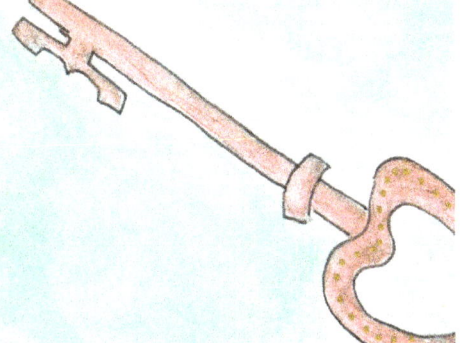

LIFE JOURNEY

There are choices in life. Not just this or that.

Take your time; take a breath to choose what and which way you want to go.

The path you chose is the map of who you are.

Choices you make light up the sky of your dreams.

That is the only real thing there is.

Other potentiality fades away in time.

You are the light bearer of your path.

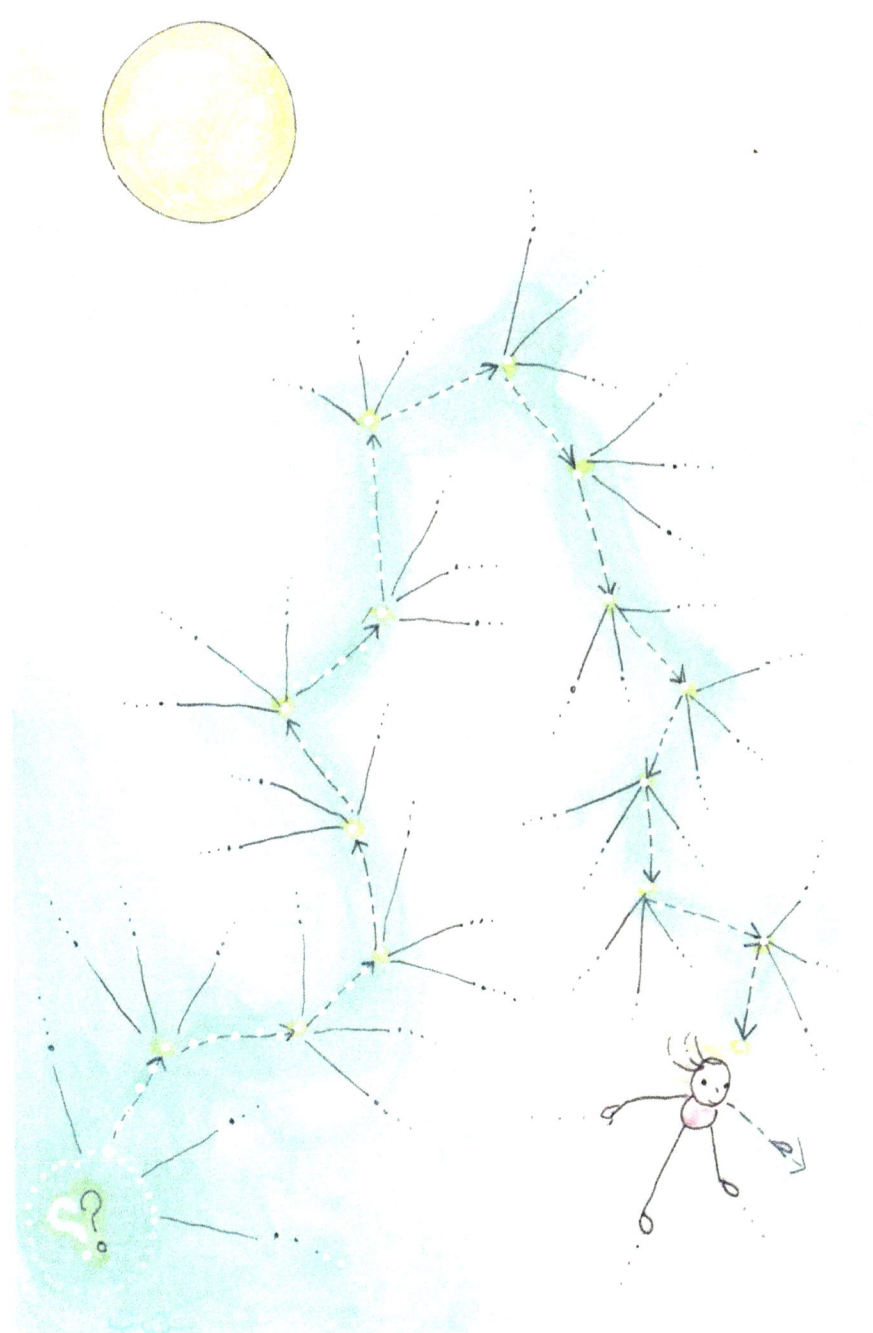

NATURAL LAW

There is Universal Law.

Ultimately, that is cause and effect.

It's as above and so below, so above as below.

Their symbiotic relationship continues to cause and affect each other.

The duality keeps experiencing one another and expands more.

Above and below, the awareness of life itself expands.

So the above and the below are now more condensed than ever before.

(Duality)

So Above

As Above So Below

more EXPERIENCE
more Expansion
The   moreAwareness
    more Condensation

As Above

So Below

As Below

(Symbiotic Relationship)

FREQUENCY

Higher frequency is lighter, more positive and more fun.

But why is that?

In the plane of higher frequency, there is more movement of the frequency, yet it is calmer and lighter than lower frequency.

It is a perfect and beautiful place to be.

It's a productive yet calming place to be.

Why is a higher frequency more balanced than a lower frequency?

Because we find balance in the space between Yin & Yang—crossing over the centre, there is the perfect point in the middle.

A higher frequency can hit this perfection point more often, as it travels a lot faster than lower frequency.

Q: Why **is** higher frequency more balanced than lower frequency?

⇒ Balance is found in the movement between Yin & Yang — cross overing the center is the perfection point.

⇒ Frequency ... higher frequency can hit this perfection point more as it travells a lot more than lower frequency.

HAPPY ECLIPSE - ALL CHANGES ARE FOR REBALANCING

During a lunar eclipse, the Earth is orbiting between the Sun and the moon. During a Solar eclipse, the moon orbits between the Sun and the Earth.

The moon and the Sun are eclipsing and rebalancing the energy of the opposite. So go with the flow and wobble with it.

This season of transition will pass when we reestablish a balance.

This shift will leave with you what is important to you.

What is meaningful for you?

What is eclipsing in your life?

Wobble, wobble and enjoy your ability to see what's surfacing.

AUTHENTICITY

Your uniqueness unfolds with love.

That is how you open each layer of petals and get to the state of pure authenticity.

Encourage the process with love.

Live the experience of seeking.

As the journey itself is the reflection of your authenticity, that is the whole self and who you are becoming.

AVATAR IN TRAINING

The Original, the authentic one, had decided to have more experiences and other versions of itself.

So we live and add more layers of different self and different lives.

The present moment in your current life is the outermost layer.

We are picking ourselves up from where we left off: in our past moments and past lives.

All the past me is inside me.

We are all AVATAR in training.

So look within. Within the thousands of lives, there is pure authenticity.

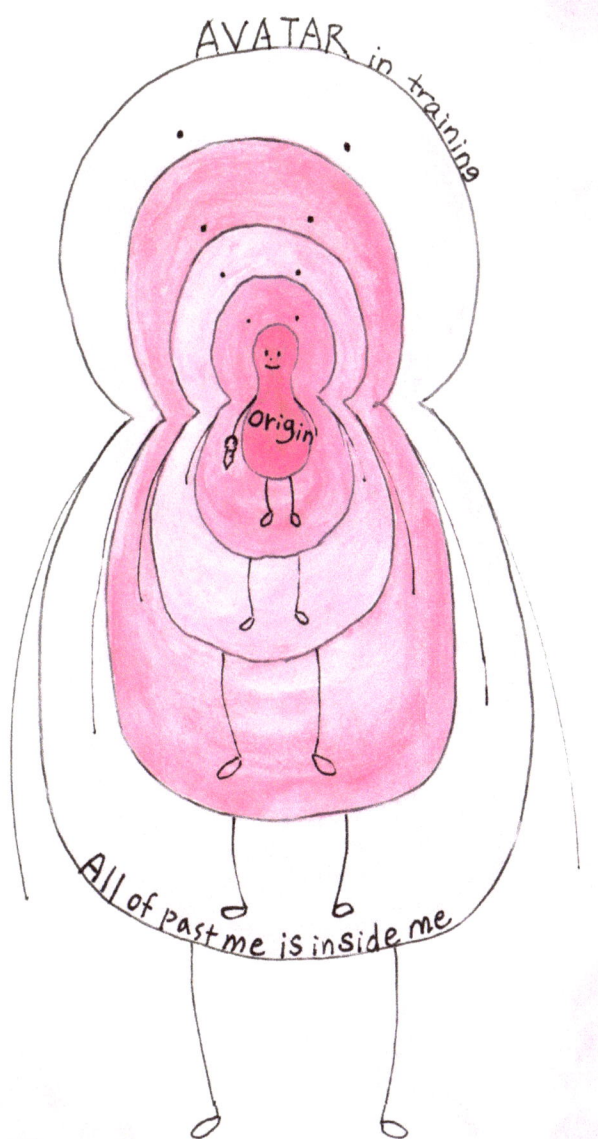

COM-PASS

Com-Pass.

Go towards where 'com' is happening.

Where is the community you like?

Who can you share a commonality with and communicate with?

Where is your compassion pulled?

Go where you can find a bundle of joy.

We are passing the past.

Go to where your heart takes you.

The pull is there.

The compass works when your heart works.

Go where your heart points you.

DOLPHINS AND A DOT

Within the self, there is Yin and Yang.

Opposites create continuous flow and circulation.

I am not alone, even within me.

There is another 'I' inside me.

I am more than just one me.

So create the flow and light up as you circulate in the motion with the multiple you.

Within the circulation of differences, there is a dot of truth.

WITHOUT DIFFERENCE, THERE IS NO BALANCE AND HARMONY

Although unaware, humans approve sameness.

In reality, it is the difference that produces the life force.

Without the difference, there is no such thing as balance.

Because the differences create motion to search for the balance, circulation continues.

And within the circulation, we find harmony.

SUCCESSFUL RELATIONSHIP

Relationships work when we commit entirely to understanding each other.

Up and down, left to right, it takes both to tango, right?

If we can enjoy the dance, we are doing it right.

I'm not the same, but I understand your needs and wants.

So here we are.

Thank you for your kindness to understand me.

It's fun that we can dance.

YIN AND YANG

Without difference, there is no balance.

Searching for balance creates circulation.

Circulation of energy creates more and more; that is expansion. That is creation.

When creation creates, it's in its element.

So when we create, we are happy.

Without difference, there is no balance. Searching for balance creates circulation. Circulation creates its initial element. Circulation of energy creates more when creation creates circulation.

INTERDEPENDANCE IS AN EXPRESSION OF ONENESS

All individuals are longing for connection with others.

It's not dependency or control that we need.

That's not fun.

What we want is 'interdependence' that is independent beings gathering to enjoy each other's company.

We find joy in celebrating ONENESS with love, music and water baths with birdies.

It's the natural state of who we are.

Be yourself and gather for fun.

We are one, and it is fun to express our ONENESS.

Yuki's Art & Language

www.yukisartandlanguage.com
 @yukisartlanguage

www.ingramcontent.com/pod-product-compliance
Lightning Source LLC
Chambersburg PA
CBHW040759150426
42811CB00056B/1086